poyms for people

poyms for people

David Galloway

Cover design by Shay Culligan

Author photograph by Bronwyn Galloway

ISBN: 978-1-952326-83-7

Kelsay Books
502 South 1040 East, A-119
American Fork, Utah, 84003

For Teresa, who doesn't like poetry
but
likes
me

Acknowledgments

American Journal of Poetry: "ten poems about my great-great-grandfather's murder"

Atlanta Review: "Night, Verbezhichi"

Chiron Review: "Lidia"

Citron Review: "My Daughter Haunts"

Comstock Review: "Thought, on Helping My Daughter Write an Ode"

Fredericksburg Literary and Art Review: "On a Street in Dublin"

Gargoyle: "how i have saved the world"

Hamilton Stone Review: "Small Talk," "electro-magnetic pulse"

Late Knocking: "Missile Silo, Jacksonville," "Buffalo Man"

Loch Raven Review: "Eyewitness," "The Gypsy Children in Orange"

New Mexico Review: "The Dentist," "Climbing Trees"

Penn Review: "why I shouldn't time travel"

Permafrost: "piroshki"

Prairie Fire: "Hillendale Country Club, Morning Guard"

Salamander: "Crossing Lake Champlain at Night"

Sky Island Journal: "Call of Nature, Mongolia"

Slippery Elm: "The Golem"

The Apprentice Writer: "Cathy"

The Finger: "Lake Straus"

The Phoenix: "orion"

Typehouse Literary Review: "January 30, 2012," "The Last Milk"

Contents

IV: parenting

V: tramping

ars poetica, or poyms for people

> the snow is soft,
> and how it squashes!
> "Galumph, galumph!"
> go my galoshes.

> Eunice Tietjens, "Thaw"

now that's poetry
before i knew what poems were
i called them *poyms*
i say it was my mother's pronunciation
but she denies it,
so maybe my innocent invention,

her favorite one rhymed:
she'd always recite eunice tietjens' "thaw."

I drew pictures with *crowns,* not crayons,
and to this day
poym
seems better, more accurate, to hold the thing
than poem
poem is pretentious, black clothes and goth misery
poyms are what they need to be
essential
alive
decorative yet pragmatic
and they are for people
for when they stop being for people
they stop being
entirely

I

prehistory

ten poems about my great-great-grandfather's murder

i: just the facts

on november 11th 1889 as he
stood facing his former best friend
(who'd accused him of harassing his wife)
on the second floor of the schoolhouse
in brownsburg my great-great-grandfather
was stabbed and while he died, broken
hunting knife blade in his backbone, his
sons shot the man who did it before
the blood was cold and put a bullet
in the man's wife as she knelt in
gunfire to tend to him.

ii: brownsburg

the turnpike's 180 degree turns are one thing
with a horse and buggy, another with a rented
chevy sonic at 55. color is gone from leaves,
drifting to dull brown, air crisp with bite
of woodsmoke that says autumn, cross-scent of
manure and wet grass, round hay bales drying on
the fields, rocks sticking through every pasture.
it is only one street, houses lean close along the
turnpike, museum just two rooms, first thing
you see is a broadsheet from the *staunton spectator
and general advertiser* pasted on foam board about
the fateful day, that day that shocked the two
hundred thirty-seven citizens of brownsburg.

that newspaper captures a world of fig syrups
and ely's cream balm for catarrh, makes you
curious about the going rate of irish potatoes,
cut loaf sugar, and adamantine candles, makes
you weep for miss mary drechsler, aged twenty
years, recently died of consumption, or the two
victims of the earth-slide at black rock ore mines
near vesuvius station, where good john pickerell
and clem doyle were killed instantly. who weeps
for them? no one, we are already caught up in
the sad tale of john thomas reeves, eighteen,
kicked by a horse and killed while hauling corn,
his parents *looked upon him as their staff in the
decline of life, for he was industrious.* god rest.

iii: dr. zachariah walker

he was crazy as a loon said colonel stilington,
walker's brother-in-law, but others said
a man of high spirits and fearless courage,
who built a career as a doctor and surgeon,
served the confederacy, wintered in florida
on occasion, but estranged his friends and
got in moods, when Bettie told him he said
if you accept an apology i will commit suicide.

iv: henry miller

a big man, a wealthy man, pushing seventy
but hardly looking it, dynasty-maker with
five sons and three daughters, his weakness
a gross familiarity to women that seemed a senile
mania, said some, with incidents mentioned
in the aftermath as townsfolk shook their heads,
my cousin has his daughter's bible, inscribed
presented to louella miller by her affectionate father.

v: the inciting incident

henry miller entered the walker house
to get a receipt from bettie, the doctor's
wife, but he *offered indignities in the
grossest manner* and though we may
chuckle at the language of 1889 it made
the doctor pace the streets with a double-
barreled shotgun and hot blood in his heart,
told his friends he would shoot henry on sight,
ambush the entire family, break the arms and legs
of all the sons, leave them on the roadside.

vi: to court, to court

enough drama, says society (but society is
about to see what real drama is), so let's get
these men to court and have them work it out,
if they can't, well, that's what peace bonds are
for, that's what jail is for, we're all civilized men.
so they bring them all together to work this
out, *we were all friends once, remember,* and
this is just a misunderstanding, easily fixed.

schoolhouse's upper room stuffed with people,
millers, walkers, supporters and gawkers,
come unarmed, the millers were told, but hell,
only if the other side is, they thought, a friend
gave them advice in confidence, frowning,
*better look out for yourselves, boys, better look out
for yourselves.* so john reese, hired man, waits
on the porch with five pistols, one for each son.

white-haired e.b. bosworth the magistrate
presides, figuring the truth about this incident
that will tear apart the town in two minutes flat,
because walker ducked into his office beforehand
and though not armed earlier he picks up his
knife and gun and brings them to the school,
it's only two in the afternoon this fine november
but by sunset three of these people will be dead.

vii: almost last words

-If you will not give the peace bond, I will have to send you to jail.
That is what I want. I will be happier in jail than out of it. Will you
let me have my dinner before I go?
-Certainly, you can have your own time to get it. I will give you the
papers and let you go to jail yourself and surrender.
I want you to grant me one request before I go. I want to slap
Henry Miller in the face for insulting my wife.
-Doctor, you can't do that here.
I am going to do it.

viii: melee

walker makes to draw his gun, the gun
he isn't supposed to have, and when
that's taken away draws the nine-inch
knife and wrestles henry miller until he's
behind him, makes contact, a good ten
strokes, eight of which on examination
will be found mortal, and the firing begins.

john reese tosses pistols through the window
like a slow-mo hollywood western, hands
reaching for well-worn grips and opening
up a storm of bullets into people and someone
walks up to bettie walker as she kneels over
her dying husband and puts a bullet point-blank
in her temple. they say it's a miller who done it.

somehow this all ends, somehow the fact that
miller is dead, walker is dying, and bettie slain,
innocent, brings an end to all this ruckus.
there is no telegraph in brownsburg, you must
go to raphine and send word to the papers in
staunton and roanoke and lexington; within the
month the story will reach california and new zealand.

imagine tomorrow, when townsfolk will peer
with shudders at the lead in walls and holes in
the stovepipe, pool of blood underneath the
bench, they'll go to walker's open house and
see him and bettie laid out, while some whisper
of lynching those millers before they come to trial
because they shot that poor defenseless woman.

ix: last words

Did I kill Miller?
-Yes.
I am satisfied. They killed Bettie and gave me a mortal wound, but
I am satisfied.

x: finis

so i drove to lexington after brownsburg,
read microfilms until my eyes burned
but nothing told me where to find
that nine-inch bowie of old hook point,
western pattern, broken, the long range
38 double-action smith & wesson,
implements of bloody revenge.

the academy was torn down long ago,
but miller's house and walker's house
still stand, and they're buried in the
same cemetery at new providence,
walk the graverows and puzzle out
who was guilty, who was innocent.
whatever the good lord might decide

the elders of new providence let them
rest in the cemetery, but forbade a service
inside; there's no policy on dealing with souls
who died by violence, the papers explained,
but that increased the scandal. the miller
boys went on trial for the murder of bettie
walker but were acquitted, and that's the end.

so great-great-grandfather wronged the
wrong man's wife and got what was coming
to him, though everyone who knew the truth
died that day. i guess it doesn't matter much
since none of this deserved death, so were
they all victims or is that just too neat a bow?

Hallowed Ground, Staunton VA

The Shenandoah Valley. I know it from blue-green
skylines on hot drives south, milk cartons in convenience
stores. Half a town from Woodrow Wilson's birthplace, along a
stone-walled cemetery and West Beverly, is my grandmother's
house, above a three way intersection with four traffic lights.
There has never been a road: the fourth light faces the house.
White with green shutters, large grey porch and rusty swing,
peeling paint, yard with ash-tree stumps. From the bedroom
window, surrounded by dusty 50's model cars, a Robert E. Lee
high school diploma, an amber stuffed crocodile,
you can see the light.

Dusty canning jars in the cellar,
black walnut tree like a shriveled dryad
shading a firewood-stuffed doghouse,
dilapidated garage and rough hedge.
Dead flies in the ceiling lamps, between the panes.
Sewing room crammed with ham radio gear.
Thornrose Cemetery guards the corner opposite,
rough tower of dull stones, dark square window on the corner.
August dark, sheets rolled down. Humidity thickening
the breeze from the ancient electric fan's unshielded blades
you could poke your fingers into real easy, all is still.

The lights on both sides are red, and green lights up,
a gust of wind, a flowing up the street,
past the cemetery to Gypsy Hill Park, where peacocks awake.
Ghosts of my grandfather, wasting away while my father
ROTC-marched on a windy hill in Blacksburg. Ghosts of my
great-uncle, half-paralyzed, weeping at Thanksgiving.
Ghosts pining for apple butter and fresh baked ham, sweet iced tea,
boulder-dotted pastures and homemade rope bridges over creeks.
The light glows red to yellow to green, as if the county saw a path
there and tried to impose order on the night ranges
of spirits that left only footprints shallow as wet leaves.

II

childing

Nympholepsy, Circa 1977

A frenzy induced by the obsession
for something unattainable, says Webster.
I wasn't old enough for slavering lusts
of gossamer winged, hourglass shaped pixies.
I dressed in plaid pants and wore an Oliver
Cromwell Roundhead haircut to Sunday School.
My life's desire was for Skylab, that
brilliant shining tin can, to flutter down
and bury itself among the trees in our
backyard. There was plenty of room—
I was sure a 747 could fit between the
Winniebergers' fence and the Pitmans' pine trees.
The neighbors wouldn't notice it, of course,
and how loud could a crashing spaceship be?
I believed in some sort of twisted common law
that if it landed in my lawn, it belonged
to me. Why would NASA want the parts? The
bubble popped at school—the *Weekly Reader* map
showed a black and white star in the Pacific near
Australia, in the ocean that bore no resemblance
to the manicured order of our backyard.

Tryouts

you go because you're told, and you're that kind of kid,
the kind who does what he's told. Fifty kids in the school
cafeteria, tables pushed back, all bouncing basketballs. You
get a ball from the huge bin and start bouncing it, the din
of fifty dribbling balls echoes off the tiled walls. It takes
ten minutes for the first ball to go up, fifty pairs of nine-year
old eyes follow it. Who knows where the adults are or what
the hell they are doing, but the ball almost touches the metal-
shielded lights twenty feet above us. Then another, and another.
You wouldn't throw it, but no one is stopping the other kids, so
why not? You throw it up, and that's when he appears. The man
grabs the ball, screams. His face contorts as if you've killed
someone. You don't remember his words, just his screaming makes
everyone stop, all the balls are silenced, no sound but him
screaming, screaming at you, and you hold the ball, trembling, not
knowing what to do as he finishes his tirade and starts a drill, you
drop the ball, stagger through whatever they do but always his
face, always the screaming, always the fifty kids. No one tells you
the guy's a jerk, he was wrong, you'll be okay, no one offers
anything, a word, not a gesture, you put your head down, you can't
call him a fucker because you don't know that word yet and oh god
you hate basketball

Cathy

The children in the neighborhood
called her Thelma Weird.
She lived with her heartsick mother
in a house built into the side of
a hill and perched on an overflowing
stream. Her nephew was a photographer
for the Smithsonian Institution, she said,
and was into bugs. Every day, she walked
her dogs up and down the hill.
"Don't let her catch you!" the kids
warned, but unheeding you would stop
near her and be trapped in a web of
tales spanning generations about her
dog's last illness or a conversation
held three weeks ago. She had no
respect for property, bringing her dog
Gretchen and other furballs onto
lawns for drinks from foreign faucets.
Her real existence was the daily walk
where she emptied the pockets of her life
to every stranger and friend who strolled
that hill, telling them about ticks,
blisters, Lyme disease.

Missile Silo, Jacksonville

Now the recreation council uses the buildings
for square dances and Little League meetings,
but the rusty barbed-wire fences overgrown
with brown thorns still stand, marked with
faded U.S. government warning signs.

Along the dusty jeep path I creep to find the
vandals' three-foot slash in the chainlink.
I run past the collapsing kennel where Danes
and Pinschers growled, across cracked cement,
by a squat white outbuilding filled with drums
of magnesium shavings for the local volunteer
fire company to douse with CO_2 foam, to the
entrance of the silent silos.

I descend a bright yellow hatchway, down
slippery rungs into dark tunnels. Flashlit
steel blast doors and barren concrete rooms
lead to a blue, fading elevator in the cavern,
red and green buttons in broken steel fuse boxes.
A thin crack of light above, and two doors to the sky.

In the first silo, the fire department built
a training ground from multicolored plywood,
a houselike maze to fill with smoke.
Beer bottles, nuclear attack pamphlets, and
a ripped *Playboy* in the second, acid smell of
urine and mustiness from the damp floor.
The third, silence like the holy of holies,
my echoing footsteps and the pale flashlight
glow on the missile's empty bed.

electro-magnetic pulse

before the internet came
i feared the pulse

because i knew
that any strategic launch

of nuclear missiles
must be preceded by

the electro-magnetic pulse
which destroys car ignitions

and sensitive defense systems
and though it can be shielded

against, it is simplicity to
to create a larger explosion

so when in 1984 my mother
slid into the bench seat of

the new maroon chevy caprice
with its big square tail lights

and turned the key, producing
nothing, not a spark, i didn't

think the engine was dead, but
gripped by panic i was frozen

in the knowledge that this
was how the world ended.

Hillendale Country Club, Morning Guard

I turn rusty tumblers, free the gates,
send a spray of droplets to the cement.
Blue-white chaise lounges float in the upper pool,
flung there by last night's storm.
A green frog scoots about in the deep end—
fifteen minutes to catch him with a skimmer
and toss him outside the waist-high chainlink.

The manager left a note—*reprime baby pool filter.*
Lifeguards drift in with biscuits and orange juice from
McDonald's, or cook omelets in the snack bar.
Between the chaise lounges they find a thick paperback
on the founding of Australia that was left out in the rain.
Thwock of golf balls on the driving range, a tank explosion
and machine gun *rat-a-tat-tat* from the empty game room.

No icemaker in the snack bar, so daily we bring ice
from the clubhouse "up top"—
if you're lucky you'll pass by the back door
as the chef carves an ice sculpture with his electric knife.
You take a double-layered garbage bag to the kitchen,
fill it with cubes, and stagger down the service drive
like a crazed Santa, spine on fire and frozen.

The swim team moves to the upper pool, its steel
sides made from a liberty ship. A guard climbs
the chair made of painted plumber's pipe to watch.
Thunk the tennis machine spits balls over the net.
Two elderly women properly attired bounce
like white pillows as the pro shouts,
"You've got to go after those low ones!"

The local alcoholic has settled in to sun herself,
alternating hard liquor with her iced tea.
A teenaged girl practices springboard dives,
emerging from the deep end she tugs her neckline higher,
black suit slick as a seal, hugging every curve,
as the guards watch through the plate-glass window
like primitive man seeing fire for the first time.

crayfish

i have burned crayfish
though it did not make me
a serial killer and i never progressed
to cats or dogs or whatever else
is next

we'd gather them slippery from
under the rocks in the creek, when
the maryland humidity pressed close
and there the shade and trickling water
made cool

my friend took a tube of binaca and
sprayed it in front of his lighter,
(don't try this at home)
which turned the crayfish
lobster-red

we only did it a few times, your honor,
it didn't become a habit, but now it's harder
to think about kid cruelty, how
we all grow accustomed
to killing

This Poem Is Not about Oysters

When I was two, two-and-a-half, my Aunt Shirley
cooked me fried oysters when we were down Staunton,
it was generally understood that I liked most anything
but everyone was surprised when I put away about ten
plump ones, smiling all the while, and didn't get sick.

So you'd think a trip to the oyster feast years later
at the Jacksonville Fire Hall would make sense, but
I wouldn't touch them, and haven't since. Not
Jacksonville, Florida, nine-hundred-thousand strong,
but Jacksonville, Maryland, eleven-thousand small.

Jacksonville sits where routes 145 and 146 meet, but
it was west on Paper Mill, east on Sweet Air for us,
Jarrettsville Pike the only road that gets fast out of town,
streaking north to the state line or south to Towson.
The four corners they made was the name of the old bar

which became an Exxon and spilled its gasoline into the wells
of sixty homes and a twenty-year lawsuit, where my favorite
ice cream shop, Watty's, closed after the spill—they had no
water, so no more root beer floats, no Saturday treat after
baseball, that side of the street just up and died.

We'd get our silver queen corn from Tommy's stand on
afternoons as the sun slanted down, cook it four minutes,
before the Safeway, before barcodes, we shopped at Carroll's
Food Market, where they rang you up by hand, dug pickles
from the barrel, and floors were wooden, not tile.

My father'd pick up his 8 penny nails at Priceless Hardware,
across from the pharmacy, to finish off the downstairs
basement or the jungle gym in back, and I'd watch the man
choose our colors over the thrum of the paint-mixer.

In middle school the brother of a girl I should have asked
out took his motorbike to where Stansbury Mill crossed
Manor road and crashed, they put a memoriam page in
the back of the yearbook and we didn't know what to say.

So you see, it's not about oysters at all.

Grand Slam

Let's just say it wasn't a great career.
I started at 6 but topped out at 12
when the guys became enormous,
their pitches screaming fireballs you'd
pay good money not to face.

But take one bright afternoon in June,
the kind that makes you recite Casey
and gets you humming John Fogerty,
when God decreed, in echoing tones,
I will give you one great moment.

I brought the battered steel bat around,
the ball took off to limitless distance,
no home run fence to clear, just grass
ending where a green field of feed corn
met perfect blue sky.

The luckless center fielder pumping
out after the ball, I slowed at every
base, thinking I'd reached as far
as I could, while coaches and teammates
shouted me on and three runners scored,

I staggered through back-slaps and high-fives
to sit, still struck, on the bench, and turned
to find my mother in the stands, where
she wasn't because she'd run to get
a couple things at Safeway.

Buffalo Man

Along Jarrettsville Pike right near the county line, as the speed
limit jumps to fifty, fields of cattle and Mr. Billingsleys' former
egg farm flash past, in the sparse woods there was an
abandoned, two story house. Its faded hardwood shingles
dropped like water from a broken faucet, the windows stared
glassless and dark, thorns and vines groped at the slanted walls.

The Buffalo Man lived there, an apparition grounded in the Cretan
Minotaur augmented with Scooby Doo cartoon villains and
late-night "B" horror flicks, a seven-foot mound of horns and
stringy hair. A fantasy, like the Black Knight who came out at the
full moon, hiding in bushes under the den window, visor down and
eyes like coals, that the curtains could barely keep away.

But unlike the Knight, this roaring beast lived a few miles away
and trooped up and down the stairs of his broken house, watching
our school bus streak orange every morning. We dreamed of
the shaggy head and yellow eyes until the day I passed and
among the frozen bulldozer tracks were a few timbers, green
broken glass, a small bundle of what may have been his clothes.

you're guessing

is what they say when you try that difficult
math problem, my father said it your father
said it, trying to make you refocus on process,
not randomness, but you don't know why
we guess, do you? because you never guessed,
you always knew, but we don't, we are in the
spotlight of a boxed room, all mirrors, no way
to find the answer, all your structure and logic
collapsing, and we just want to get out, get out
of this, so we say is it sixteen? is it b^2? is it $2x+7$?
and all of those are wrong, so you say *you're
guessing* but what we are really saying is *save me*.

Archaeology 101

We've reached clay now,
and continue our tunnel to China,
digging in a wasteland where
green is nonexistent.
Metal shovels sound hollow
against the flesh of the earth.
Artifacts found—doll-like miniatures,
forgotten idols—we reverence them.
Tired, we rest and survey our progress.
"This will not work," says my companion
in disgust, "the sides keep falling in."
"Well," I say in defeat,
"then we should have started
outside the sandbox."

why I shouldn't time travel

In fourth-grade band I played the trumpet
mainly because my father had a trumpet

and so I had a trumpet, not knowing that
convenience and great art seldom go together,

what I wanted, deeply wanted, was to play the
drums, but those who were going to play

had to go into another room, and that was too
much for me, shyness matched my desire,

so I was a trumpet player for six middling years,
never excelling, always watching the drums

and those who played them, so that if I could
go back then I would not tell my earlier self to

choose the drums, I would not intervene, stealing
the trumpet before I was even born, instead

I'd show up the day the drumfolk went into the
other room and would walk up to the pudgy

trumpet player watching them and without a
word of explanation would beat him bloody,

leave him gasping on the tiles spit-ridden from
that disgusting brass instrument and vanish into

time as they called the police, so that he'd suffer
but gain nothing from his suffering, and leaving

over his tears, nothing else of the time-stream touched,
because I have already created a son who in my time

is ten times the drummer I could have ever been,
which is what I would whisper to that lost

little boy as he lay crying, huddling, unable to
understand the unjust pain of his terrible world.

Hallmark

when my alcoholic aunt got her due
from the cancer growing in her gut
teenage me sent her a card, not a get well
card, because people don't get well from
what she had, but i sent one that seemed
right, it said *in deepest sympathy,* because
that's what it felt like, i sympathized, since
though she was an alcoholic i didn't learn
that until later, besides alcoholics are people
too even if they get angry and slap their
daughters, and she always gave me nice gifts
at christmas and invited us to their motel
in ocean city and made me a sandwich from
my uncle's deli just a block from the boardwalk.
so i sent it and when they opened it, the other
aunts there to help, they thought someone was
being cruel until they saw my name, and said
oh he doesn't understand. my mother told me
this, but the shame of being wrong has far
outlasted the sense of loss at my aunt's death,
and i still think the best sentiment when you've
gotten that diagnosis is *in deepest sympathy.* in
sympathy for the world that is shit, for the
disease that will kill you, and for the fact that
you are the one who has to live it until the end.

III

adulting

Climbing Trees

If someone should ask me
When did you last climb a tree?
I would say
last Thursday, at five in the afternoon,
and I was terrified.

I pass it everyday on my after-work-walk,
until one day I think, *I should climb it.*
It demands to be climbed: a great spreading deciduous crown
downhill from the chapel by the Lee Building, in whose shadows
I once waited for candidate Al Gore (who never showed).
It overlooks the Route, Fraternity Row's white columns, the
mad rush of traffic.

The first branch is six feet high.
It's been years, since the old house,
pines leaving sap on hands, rubbing sand to scrape it off,
perfectly formed maples down the hill, dogwood on the front lawn.
I look around, see if anyone is watching.
Tuck shirt in shorts, keys in sock by ankle, swing legs and gasp.
Hands shaking, feet unsure on ant-scurrying rough bark, blinking
at the distant grass, lips dry, muscles taut.

Not like a child.
Not quick and scurrying, to escape the "It" in tag,
not fluid leaping from branch to branch, never looking down.
A breeze, the tree whispering, through the canopy people walking,
the waning sun, as my heartbeat slows I dare to turn in the perch
between three rising trunks.

There's a red abrasion on my forearm, the toll for this climb.
But it's worth it, for some reason, to be perched in the branches,
so that you wonder why you ever stopped—
as if we ever had reasons to climb in the first place,

so I suppose to the definitions of old age we might add
old age is a failure to climb trees.

The Dentist

i have never had a cavity
so the tension builds every visit
to an unendurable crescendo,
nerves twanging, flinching
the hygienist scrapes metal down my gums
sound like cracking enamel
poster of white people racing boats
try, and fail, to disassociate

i brush enough, you'd think
(my record speaks for itself, thank you)
but still my mouth fills with blood,
i know the lecture on flossing,
i stop her before she winds the glossy strands
ready to garrote the victim, beg off
to avoid her cracking my jaw open
to get at molars no one ever bothers with

raised on maryland well water,
my suspicious mother wouldn't let me
take fluoride treatments in elementary school,
i drank a gallon of milk a day
or so i claimed to friends, so that,
genetics, or stupid luck has made me this
dental superman, but all it feels like
is a curse

no one understands my fear
my daughter says vaccinations are worse
i'd trade a million shots in my upper deltoid for
this agony of expectation, because one day
it will happen, so twice a year I stagger out
gums sore, my exiting prayer that I will die
five and three-quarter months
after my last appointment

After

for J

i know a boy who jumped
we chase the how because we
will never find a why
even though the how
churns our stomachs
hits us when we least expect
like hot bronx pavement

Chess Games

Loss: My grandfather beat me in five moves on the back patio.
When he died, my mother gave me one of his chess sets,
turquoise and green pieces my uncle brought back from Vietnam,
tucked in it is a newspaper made of incomprehensible squiggles.

Win: I beat Rajiv David at the first chess club meeting—
he underestimated the dorky white kid in plaid,
after I took his queen he jerked back to focus
but it was too late. I never beat him again.

Loss: I played a lockstep sacrifice with Andrei Kabanov
in January until we were down to three pieces, just the king for me,
he said I played like a woman, which gave me angry motivation,
but not enough to win while the snow piled outside the house.

Win: I play my son on the set I got him for his eleventh birthday.
Inside the case we keep a folded yellow notepad with all our
matches. A tally mark total shows I'm ahead, for now, but each
time it gets harder, each time my mistakes cost me more.

Loss: an eleven year old at a summer camp in the Altai beat me
while I tried to expound on everything American. He did not listen.
He watched the game, while I struggled he held victory in his eyes.
He knew he was going to win before I sat down.

That is the only way to play.

the geography lesson

at a retirement party we met her
hale German woman of eighty-five
after the *what do you do* and
how do you know Susanne she told us

how at eight years old, december
forty-one, she'd hidden on the stairs
while her mother and sisters listened
to the declaration of war on the US,

and when the broadcast finished,
turned off the radio, brought out the
faded world atlas, and found the
belligerent nation the führer had

just condemned to death. Fingers
pointing, tracing, and instead of
questions, silence, looks at each other
no one willing to say it until a year later

when her mother would clutch her close
as the red army began to pour from the east
saying, *the only way you and i will survive
is if we lose this war*

Thought, on Being Fired

when you're asked to meet
the president it is usually a
good thing, but notice, be
aware of what the secretary
does not say—just that *they'd*
like to meet with you

so you, happy little idiot,
walk in and sit down and
only then does the sliver of
doubt start, the last resistant
flexing of the epidermis before
the needle slides home

reeling, gaping, leaving in a blur
(you thought you were getting a
commendation), you drive home
in a haze, thinking so hard you
forget to drive into the grille
of the oncoming semi

a forty-five mile commute
produces no eloquent defense,
no report that is not grim
because home is no refuge,
it's a wife and three children
and one non-existent income,

your hopelessness checked
by a smart woman who says
to fight, and you do, forgetting
how ready you were to lay down,
die in that moment, give it up
to be what they say you are

you win—it takes a year,
a year of making kill lists at
each flip turn at the Y, of
running into perpetrators
hundreds of miles from home
as if you're starring in a bad sitcom.

it is the best, almost miraculous
considering others after you who
lose, who vanish, but on some days
still you only want to feel that gun
in your hand, helping you with
your bloody arithmetic

Eyewitness

"It was Grace!"
I shout and stumble out of sleep gasping
human-warmed air, half out of bed,
thin stream of cold flowing over the sill,
flapping venetian blinds in a metallic clatter,
clock numbers neon green and wavering
as I move my jaw.

5:00 a.m.

Chase the dream meaning, breathe fast,
think, run after the last visual snatches
slipping away like butterflies.

The poster of Rodin's *The Kiss* illuminated
by a brief headlight in the windowpane,
a distant siren, rush of wind and tree shadows.

I talk in sleep. Roommates heard Russian
from my pillows, arguments and conversations
I can't remember and wanted to tape.

I yelled on a camping trip to Rodney,
rose up shouting "Fall in!" from my bunk
but no one moved in metal cots creaking
and smoldering breath of the wood stove's
fire dying, brilliant moonlight on the snow.

I know it was Grace, I know like a true prophet.
It was horrible, I was involved, and I know
it was Grace.

Once I grabbed you in sleep, maybe chasing Grace.
Silent and warm, you stole the quilts and sheets,
tight dark ringlets falling on your cheek. As I
crawl back, still chasing Grace, a soft hand moves
out of sleep and around me. A murmur, a kiss, and
          I have rediscovered
                grace

Thought, on grading exams about vampires

it's a serious class, don't give me that
anti-ivory tower skepticism,
save that for wine appreciation,
basket-weaving, or zombies

we read a lot and yes watch movies
and a little *Buffy* but in the end
they must pass three multiple choice
exams, which are the funnest to write

I put in distractors meant to give you
a chuckle except too many students
pick them, and it's hard to face a group who
agreed that the original name of Dracula was

Count Chocula

Permanence

in the same way that after
watching a television program
about horrific accidental amputation
you reach down to touch your leg
assure yourself it's still there and whole

the news of our neighbors' marital separation
delivered via unstamped letter to the doorstep
made us both pause, feeling thankful then guilty
but more aware of what was still between us
and what was forever broken for them

Lake Straus

In 1948 they dammed Broad Creek, making the lake.
My uncle camped here forty years ago, watched
concrete poured, timbers cut and fitted, the span
above built by eager Seabees. This spring they
opened the dam to rebuild the bridge, for weeks
the drained bed lay bare, mounds of drying sludge
crisscrossed by the thin channel, until the dam was
closed and the water rose.

Wasted topsoil from a thousand farms chokes the lake,
thick on its bottom. You can almost walk across now.
The dam cannot be opened to release the mud each
season; downstreamers' complaints and legal motions
close it better than the huge steel screw, its floodgate
jammed opened a crack with massive tree trunks
from the last flood.

Canoes and rowboats settle closer each year
to the soft muck. A pole poked down brings
up green algae clumps, oars and paddles
get stuck and we find them, days and weeks later,
just under the surface, dim orange plastic ghosting up.

In the summers the water reeks, mixed with the heat,
and after swamping their crafts canoeists rush to shower
at the pool. The staff talks about DDT, glowing fish,
and sticky mud like a man joking about cancer
the day before he dies.

Fifty-eight acres of watershed are evolving to grassy field;
soon there will be no aquatics at the waterfront; a waterfront
will cease to mean a lake, a place of great waters.
There will be no front and no behind,
no shallow and no deep.

Acting, in fatigues

i laced up my borrowed boots
in the hot july of '98, drove to
fort drum in a rattling humvee convoy
to train with delta company,
2nd battalion, 108th infantry,
new york army national guard.

after the range, where the fifty-cal
shredded my ears, they chose me to
simulate gas poisoning, the captain
gave me my assignment and i led the squad
around the dusty hill for a supposed training
exercise, then slowed, stopped.

asked to catch my breath, their expressions
doubting the mettle of this new guy who couldn't
walk fifty yards without a rest break, until it dawns
on them three seconds later and they mask up
in panic as the sergeant gasps
fuck, it's a symptom!

Crossing Lake Champlain at Night

Our directions said take exit 31 or 33
so we of course took 32 and drove off the map
into thin grey roads, slanting drizzle, pairs of Rottweilers
guarding driveways from our turnarounds
until we reach it, a small pier, a tiny building.
We buy a ticket and slide in behind the only other car,
cut the engine. All you can hear is the slap-bump
of the floating docks across the way
the silence of slow-dripping rain
waiting as only a ferry can make you wait,
waiting as if on the final outward breath of a prayer.

Small Talk

I saw the woman damaged, standing in line, as
I waited for my children to retrieve a 500 count
package of napkins we forgot on the first pass.

Flashing lights a block away suggested an accident.
She wore fresh bandages on her arm, a livid scrape
on her forehead, bloody nicks everywhere else.

She reached the cashier, a young girl with a ponytail,
who dazzled a smile and asked, *how are you today?*
pushing *good, well, great* despite all the evidence.

And the woman battered played the game, saying
fine, thank you on that horrific day when all went bad,
took her snack bars and soda and winced out the door.

i will not be climbing everest

If you climb a mountain for the first time and die on the descent, is it really a complete first ascent of the mountain? I am rather inclined to think personally that maybe it is quite important, the getting down, and the complete climb of a mountain is reaching the summit and getting safely to the bottom again.
—Sir Edmund Hillary

we focus on the upward vector
that is fame and thrill and machismo,
i grant the strength of will and body,
but i will not be climbing everest
this year, or any year, so put your
mind at rest. though i respect those
who do—no, sorry, you are insane,

mother nature took away all warmth
and air on the peak so no one would
climb it, but you strap technology and
oxygen to your body and trudge upwards.
i have no wish to lose my nose, cheeks,
extremities to say i have stood on the roof
of the world, though i hear the view is pretty.

you say it is a thrill, but so are hard drugs
which have just as much risk of death,
you cite george mallory, who climbed it
because *it is there,* but he IS there—
frozen a hundred years on the north face,
identified by a tag on his clothing like
a kindergartner on the first day.

i'll stick to poky hills promising a
minor tumble, my ability to climb peaks
tapped out at six, when my parents
took me to rocks state park and had me
pose near the cliff edge, not near enough to
be unsafe but in my unsmiling face
you can almost see the trembling.

Lidia

for Lidia Samukowicz Pacira, 1934-2016

You know what is, she'd say at the
beginning of a thought, and at the end,
with Old Testament authority, she'd finish,
and so! with a sage nod, hands spread

For a woman so educated, with a doctorate,
fluent in English, Russian, Polish (if not more),
that moment of ungrammatical lightness
in her speech always made me smile

She'd tell me *what is* over batter-dipped apples
fried in oil, topped with blueberry sauce
or honey we'd eat in her kitchen, by the
living room festooned with plants

She told me *what was,* when in April fifty-two
the KGB shattered the family, exiled them
to Kazakhstan *forever*—using those exact words
(the Soviets did not joke with time)

They picked cotton under guard, froze in
winter and burned in summer, just eleven months
later the red king was dead and freedom, of a sort—
but no return, still the dust of Central Asia

Her father sickened and died in the very cancer ward
that Solzhenitsyn later made a book of, but after four
years the rest returned to Poland, not quite whole, but
survivors of the Soviet experiment's excesses

In the nineties the wheel spun round, ex-prisoners
rehabilitated, labeled *groundlessly repressed for
political reasons,* but that was not even an apology,
no attempt to make right, so every suffering was futile

She told me this as the *kielbasa* fried and crackled,
browning on the stove, and I watched as tears started
in her eyes when she spoke of her father, but never fell,
seeping, vanishing back into a catalog of old pain

how i have saved the world

see how I have saved the world.
when our dishwasher died, they
pulled it out of the cabinetry and
in those five minutes of access i
peered under the space that had not
been peered at since the house
was built in turbulent sixty-eight.

behind the lazy susan was a glass
cookie jar. it could only have been
put there deliberately, and the only
reason is that it is cursed. i will not
open it, never fear. it is glass, but
only *looks* like it is empty. there are
many things that look like nothing.

my best guess is a pestilence, a world-
killing virus secreted under my cabinet.
i will not have that on my hands, and
i wish the former owners, that mild-mannered
seventy-odd couple, she a housewife, he a
local bank and trust manager, had warned us,
had told us of the evil they had contained

so that we could be on our guard. but we are
lucky, for it was i who found it, i who will
do the right thing now. i will put the cookie
jar in a box in the attic, tightly sealed with
the best strapping tape, with *do not open until
the end of the world* written on it in capitals
with big black marker, and we will all be safe.

you're welcome.

take that billy collins

i don't like facebook because i know it's
all russian bots looking at me through my
laptop camera but still i go to see if anyone
is doing anything interesting, and better than
me, and i see that billy collins is teaching classes
on poetry, which is something he is very
qualified to do, this is no trump university here
but he starts by saying poetry does not need a story
that's not what its function is and my ears perk
up like the animals he suggests are good to read
poetry to but my thought is not *yes, indeed* my
thought is *no, no, no* because story is everything
and everything is story and even a tiny haiku is
a story about a feeling and even that, even this,
is a story so take that billy collins take that

January 30, 2012

For A.T.

You lived at the other end of Lavale,
a one-eighth mile dead end,
enough incline to coast down
on our bikes with just a pedal or two.

You owned a succession of liver-spotted
dogs named Winston with Roman numerals
after their names, like medieval kings,
so many I can't remember the final incarnation.

We'd hike to the creek to catch salamanders,
pluck Japanese beetles from the rose bushes
and set them on wood-chip rafts in the rain barrel,
or try and fail at luring a robin under our box-trap.

In 4th grade we went on a coloring kick, filling
blank sheets with pages from our future
magnum opus, *Animals of the World,* but only
finishing *Volume One: Birds.*

Your unpublished classic, "Ten Army Friends,"
I have in first edition mimeograph.
Our posse fought a mythical war while listening to
Top 40 hits of the late 1970's in our tanks.

In middle school a different crowd, cigarettes,
a note to your girlfriend with sketches of marijuana plants
pulled us apart, we moved off like the silk of milkweed
pods we'd dissect and throw into the breeze.

But not a break, really, more a pause,
fifteen years later at that wedding we met
again for the last time, you took my cell
number to call when I was in town.

When the news of a man trapped
beneath the car he'd been working on
ripped through my mind it felt like
every good memory was burning.

IV

parenting

The Golem

Sit still. Try to control your breathing,
for this will be painful. Not only the
body, but mind and mythical heart
as well. Because we like to know what
will happen, even though knowing
itself is painful, we crave it ever since
Eve passed the fruit to Adam's willing
hand. I will take the best parts of you,
and the worst, both those you see and
those that are hidden. I will mix them
so that you do not know which is which,
but will be ever surprised. I will dig my
fingers deep into this raw clay, driving
it under my fingernails, ripping and
tearing it through violence and chaos into
something new, that will think and walk
and breathe on its own. It will neither love
nor hate you, at first, but everything you do,
everything you say, every action of your life
until your last breath will change it, will
lead it in return to imitate emotions, and
you will never be able to predict the outcome.
If someday it should turn on you, beware, for
it knows all your weaknesses, and can kill with
a single word, can rip you inside out with pain.
For the thing I have created, the golem of your
flesh, will be all things to you, but never will
be simple, never will be uncomplicated, for
that is the natural, unadorned state of the thing
we call a child, and merely calling it your child
is the one act that will never make it yours.

Thought, on Watching My Daughter Born
Underwater

If I were an ignorant child,
I might think that babies came
from bathtubs after seeing this.
Two people got in, one in green scrubs,
one buckling from pain,
and then there were three.
A baby rose up through the waters
as if a magic trick had been performed,
as if the midwife waved her hands
said a prayer to the goddess of childbirth
and was given a new soul and body to
bring out of water, from whence we all came,
and into air to breathe and walk and live.

Miracles

I ask you: what is a miracle if not the manifestation
of light where darkness is expected?
                                        —Leigh Ann Henion

oh let me testify
to a blustery october, my wife
takes our five-year-old boy
to buy a special mylar balloon,
a big blue shark, the perfect decoration
for his birthday party, but as she's
bundling the other balloons
like a resistant squid into the van
a willful gust tears the shark balloon
away. though it bears a small weight
that keeps it from ascending straight to
heaven it is now fifteen feet in the air, fleeing
as the boy cries after it, stung by the speed of
loss and unfairness, of barely being able to
have before it is *gone.*

I hear of this at home while packing the cake
and juice, load my daughter in the car, as we
pass the store say, *let's just see if we can find*
it, as if the gods of wind would be so kind as to
return what they stole. we drive up to find a
twenty-foot straggly maple by the crumbling
fencerow has caught a flying shark in its limbs.
Not too far out of reach, just enough that on tiptoe
I can bring it down, undamaged, iridescent and
blue and crinkly and sharky beyond belief,
my daughter cheers because children always
recognize the miraculous before we do.

though I be a hard-hearted atheist who shucked
presbyterianism something melts at this small
miracle, something so primal that a thousand
years ago I'd build a stone shrine at that sacred
maple trunk, dwelling place of the spirit called to
be our family protector, light a candle there on the
anniversary of the day our shark was returned to us,
leave a loaf of bread at sunset and depart, bowing,
face full of tears and glory at the spirit's small miracles.

Swimming at Taughannock

Dawson Hill is missing.

Lifeguards clear the swimming area.
On the diving dock fifty yards out,
six people watch, uncomprehending,
blinking in the sun.
We wait on our maroon blanket
kids safely with us
as the bathrooms,
the playground,
the parking lot
are checked.
The loudspeaker barks every few minutes,
my four-year old keeps asking when we can swim again.
The lifeguards make a first pass through the shallow area,
walking,
then get out the fins and masks and start their search dives,
diving, surfacing
diving, surfacing.
Through minutes ticking past
until Dawson Hill is found
safe
on the boat dock by his dad,
I'm not so much noticing all these things
as how with minutes stretching on and no sign of him
my wife struggles
to keep
from
weeping.

My Daughter Haunts

My daughter haunts the house like
a quiet poltergeist, moving through rooms
leaving markers that she's been there.
When her brother falls asleep she discards
her bed for his, and begins her work.

We find him, hair smeared with vaseline,
trash can upended, a million used kleenex flooding
the floor, recycling containers strewn
in the kitchen, as if a spirit had sought
the emptiness in each milk carton.

Her magnum opus: stealing the purple scissors
trimming both her hair and his
but neatly placing shorn locks in the trash can
and returning the scissors to their place so
it took us three days to discover the crime.

Then she perches, supine, on the mound of bedclothes,
divested of the encumbrances of clothing and diapers,
sometimes with her brother's stolen pillow under her,
signature thumb in mouth,
tasks completed until the dawn.

The Last Milk

My youngest daughter is thirteen.
We still have four ounces of breast milk
for her in the freezer in a tiny plastic bottle.
This is no odd totemic hold-over,
like keeping a piece of her caul,
it is simple neglect, really.
It is first forgetting, then remembering,
then finding in the rush of things.

The bottle has outlasted two refrigerators
and still sits, semi-lost, on the bottom of the freezer.
But every time the appliance dies we try,
but fail, to do something with it.
There is no earthly reason for this.
It is no good to anyone. But it is, after all, a totem.
Despite not wanting to be one,
sometimes things become totems on their own.

It speaks to mid-morning feedings,
upset stomachs and burping over the shoulder,
the visual absurdity of a breast-pump,
but also to a perfect upturned face and
tiny nostrils as close as two humans can be.
We will never throw it out. I know that.
When we are gone, the children will find it
when they empty our freezer, and wonder why.

So read this.

The Examination

I have a question
if someone is strong enough to punch through a wall
are they strong enough to punch through a refrigerator?
if you know what you are doing you will avoid such questions
but it's much too late for that
a ten-year old boy is hanging on the other end
impatient at your slow processing of this verbal insanity
as you get lost in trivialities
> what kind of wall?
> what kind of refrigerator?
> why is all this punching taking place?
because it is unanswerable,
you have failed your significant examination,
better luck next time
(for there will so be a next time)
but because you did not answer correctly
in approximately forty-seven seconds
your interrogator is going to
simply explode.

Thought, on Helping My Daughter Write an Ode

The yam tendril grows as rapidly as you

she writes, I tell her to take out words,
slim it down, turn from prose to verse,
let the image shine.

She hesitates, torn between listening to me
and her 9th grade English teacher, not sure
my version works, that it succeeds as an
ode on *Things Fall Apart*.

I'm the only one who picked an ode

she mumbles, wondering at her decision,
sprawled on the sofa, two purple pigtails hanging down
face scrunched, concentrating, on this impossible task
and this ridiculous form.

She snaps the laptop together with a snort,
done for the night, flounces off to pick a more logical subject,
I savor the wonderful line, whispering it to emptiness,
hoping it makes the cut—

a yam tendril grows as you.

orion

she got a tattoo at nineteen
which is better than fourteen
but still seems to me rushed

dithered over the design and
chose the star-pattern we showed
her, night after childhood night

she pointed out the hypocrisy
of claiming she'd marred her
perfection by charging us again

with not having gotten proper
stitches for the time she barreled
into a chair at age two and cut her

eyebrow, producing a scar she
laments on a daily basis, mending
it with makeup before going out

the tattoo made her happy,
which parents profess to want
but collided with my happiness

though i cannot love it
i can her, but if I ever had to
identify her by that constellation

i am sure those lines would
finally shatter
the broken pieces of me

In a Quiet Hour

I sent a set of poems to a colleague and she wrote
I will read them tomorrow, in a quiet hour

These hours occur when people leave the house,
and by people I mean three loud, often-angry teens,
the kind you alternately admire for their adult qualities
but loathe for their volume, their cussing, their selfish
pursuit of our money and time and cars, jockeying
nightly to see who gets the ancient blue Prius tomorrow.

When the sink broke, they washed dishes in the
basement, over the ceramic clang you could hear them
argue about who did more, who was slacking, they'd
segue into group shout-singing the latest pop song, but
soon back to bickering, a living video manual on *homo*
sapiens adolescenta ages fourteen to nineteen.

Now they have all gone, the oldest to waitress at
at the New Orleans supper club downtown, the
boy to his girlfriend's house to canoodle, where her
family seems content to feed him daily, youngest
technically here, but locked in self-imposed
exile in a bedroom so messy we have given up.

My wife takes a walk in late afternoon sunshine,
I sit here and the quiet descends. I can do things
in this time, but as the quiet hour stretches on,
I know that if I wait long enough all I will crave is
the return of bustle, of clatter, of voices and bodies.
If silence is death, noise is life. Let there be noise.

V

tramping

call of nature, mongolia

this family moves four times a year, dismantles the hut,
packs everything and sets off for the next season's destination,
leaves behind the fencing, herds the flocks ahead of them,
their dogs keep the mass of bobbing future wool intact.

russians say *yurta* which gives us our *yurt,* but mongolians
say *ger* which means *home.* from the one nearby hill, topped
with a prayer flag and rock mound, the *ger* below squats
like an uncooked white biscuit in a green sea.

inside, the stove has pride of place in center, three beds against
the outer walls, rug-covered ground, hardly enough places
to store what you'd need, you think, but you are distracted
by the red meat hanging by the doorway, curing for later.

mother prepares milk-tea and bowls of noodles mixed
with mutton, father serenades with the two-string *topshur,*
but eventually a missing object teases your mind: since the
ger is the only thing built for miles, and you ask because you

must, *so where...?* and the answer is, you go away. there is
no need for little privies to sanctify this act which is, after all,
nothing special, humans have been blessing or despoiling the
earth for two hundred thousand years, kings and peasants both.

you go away until your soul is satisfied. everyone knows where
you go, and will not walk or look that way until you return.
you must take all your supplies with you, because your destination
is a patch of grass indistinguishable from any other patch,

a patch that was training ground for world conquest, not
as if a great khan and his horde will ride up these days
(but on the other side of the nearest hill is a new genghis statue),
grass unmarred by trees, silence undisturbed by birds, for

there are no trees for birds to perch in, you can see only
high soaring hawks who make no sound. my soul is satisfied
about a hundred yards from the *ger,* when you stop walking
because to walk any further will serve no purpose, and is absurd.

you crouch on the endless mongolian plain; nascent agoraphobia
at work, missing your nine square feet of traditional space, walls
and privacy and the modern consolation that no one can see you,
to compensate you survey all compass directions like a lost sailor,

when it is time to walk back you do so feeling like the brunt
of a practical joke, the *ger* draws closer again, papa's motorcycle
parked by the east side, the sheep and goats muttering in their pen,
and the dogs rush to greet you as if you're coming home from war.

Coming Out of Lenin

They say he's only 78% real, now, but that
still demands a visit, 78% of what he was requires
a look, besides you never know how long he'll lie
here, any day they could trundle him off and put
him in the ground like his wife demanded back in
1924, no longer a waxy representative of the revolution.
It's January, but still we wait forty minutes to pass
metal detectors and descend into the mausoleum,
the shushing guards have no effect on a rickety
Russian lady ahead of us, who mutters as if making
incantations to bring Ilych to life. Outside, bright air
and crisp wind, a young man spits on Stalin's grave
while the guards drag him away and people watch
like spectators, aka building blocks for dictators.

Baikal Perspective

i have swum the deepest, oldest lake in the world,
but *swum* makes it sound as if i cavorted with
the chubby, adorable *nerpa,* baikal's freshwater seal,
when in fact I dipped my fragile self in the frigid waters
and fled

we took a cadre of eager students halfway across
the world, to olkhon island in the middle of baikal,
where in june the icy tips of the distant primorskii range
still sit snow-capped, glinting across the small sea,
its water a striking forty-two degrees fahrenheit

they trundled a blue truck with a wood-fired
mini-sauna on back to the rippling edge,
parked it on the sand so after each dip
we could retreat to a sanctuary of
smoldering beech and pine

we ran, stepping into liquid nitrogen,
burying our heads beneath one-fifth of the world's
fresh water that pooled here only twenty-five
million years ago, emerged frozen and staggered
to the truck until warmth returned

we march to the dining hall, the serving lady
asks if we swam, *yes* we say *yes,* proud at
braving this extremity of nature, but she slings
our hot lunch plates to the table with a pitying glance
as she returns to the kitchen, saying

I swim it every day

Tmutarakán

There is not a better name, no better combination
of sounds in the world, please savor it, don't rush
to disregard it as unpronounceable, it is well within
your talents, and I've given you a stress mark to help.

The *tmu-* a delightful combination, why don't we have
it in English? I can see innumerable words improved
by an initial *tmu-*. But above all, the *tmu-* makes us
realize we are not in Kansas anymore, linguistically.

—*tarakan,* like the name of an invented world, or
a Narnian lord. *Taraka* means *protector* in Hindi,
so we have sounds that make us think of other
sounds, ways in which this word sparkles in dark.

The Ionian colony named *Hermonassa* grew here,
and from the sixth century Grecians, Bulgars, Huns,
Khazars, Jews all walked these streets, where the Byzantines
gathered naptha to make liquid fire, destroyer of navies.

The Arabs called it Samkarsh, that is not bad, but no
Tmutarakan. In the eighteenth century it fell into ruin,
but how could a place with this name fall into ruin? A
name that good should provide protection, a holy shield.

Russian has enshrined it in an idiom—to go to Tmutarakan
is to go to an obscure, godforsaken place. But it is not. I
will go, I am packing my bags now. Meet me there, at the
end of the world, we will crouch on the sand and look across

the Kerch Strait, ignore the Crimean Bridge and oil tankers
passing, instead look for broken stones, excavations that
continue through meters of slag because here history is
deep, here where Tmutarakan was, and is, and will be.

Linguistically Hobbled, Pontorson

she wanted to stay with the laundry,
though i didn't speak french and she did,
something about jeans that needed
to be washed, a certain unwillingness to
walk in public in pajama pants, besides,
looking at it fourth-dimensionally
i will have to live at least twenty-five
years with this woman, so no arguing.

she gave me two coins of the four we needed
to run the machines and the phrase of power
comme ça
        like this
and so armed i set forth to obtain change.

i ventured to the nearest grocery store,
stood patiently in line behind people buying
real things needed for real lives
not tourists
baguettes, cheese, cured ham, bright greens,
empty-handed except for my coins came
to the cashier, held out my palm, one with a bill,
the other with my token coins, pointed, said
comme ça?

it only took ten minutes for her to understand
what i needed.

i did not have, it turned out, a phrase of power,
the cashier thought i was an idiot,
although i cannot prove this since i am no mind-reader
and *je ne parle pas français* to boot but her
expression was a textbook example
of the international language
of scorn.

Pechka

Добра та речь, что в избе есть печь.
Conversation is good if there is a stove in the hut.

let me introduce you to the russian stove, the
péchka, a massive white-plastered brick cube
taking up a quarter of the *izba,* the log hut.
it's at least six feet high and since the firebox
sends the heat through channels and flues
until it exits the chimney, there is no griddle,
no hot surface, you can sleep on top if you
lay down a good mattress and blankets,
the ambient heat warms you from below,
better than the seats in any high-end sedan.

twenty years ago zinaida stepanova built this
hut herself and the *bánya* next door, which has
been heating all day for us to use as night falls.
andrei sergeevich and i enter, take turns
beating each other with *véniki,* leafy birch
branches, fragrant but whiplike when wet,
when swung by someone who means it.
we steam, then run into the winter outside,
stand there with heat pluming, rising to
infinity and stars, melting the snow around us.

zinaida stepanovna makes *yózhiki,* meaning
little hedgehogs, meat dumplings with cooked rice
the grains poking out like the spines of the *yózh,*
the hedgehog, that is likely hibernating nearby
instead of scurrying around the stacked firewood
by the back door, a dozen yards from the water-well,
firewood you have to walk three miles to cut from
the forest with a sled bouncing behind you, no
problem for the septuagenarian women of the
village, who survived the war and soviet power.

there is no meal like the meal after a *banya*.
going to banya on a full stomach is not good,
so use your mother's commandment about not
swimming and add four or five hours. well
steamed we sit to eat, the little hedgehogs
vanish but are instantly replaced, and when
done zinaida stepanova points to the top
of the stove and a thick pile of blankets and
pillows and asks, *do you want to take a nap?*
if i had not, i could not write this, so yes.

The General

St. Petersburg, 2007

He was dining with his friend,
Vanya of the bandaged hand
in the back room of Kish-Mish,
the Azeri restaurant on Nekrasov Street
amid exotic fish tanks, red and gold sofas,
photographs of old Baku.

He orders eight bottles of champagne,
peeling bills from a wad of thousand-ruble notes.
Muscular and balding, greying hair cut close,
thin line of black mustache, he refuses to be photographed,
my only evidence a sneaky shot someone snapped
from almost underneath the table.

We're half a block from the Puppet Theater hostel,
me and my seven students, their Russian as bad
as his English. I count the minutes as they chug the gifted
champagne, nursing mine, waiting to see
if this fifty-year old man will actually hit
on American coeds.

He arm-wrestles Shane,
drinks from a wineglass balanced on his elbow,
takes Ellen on his knee and has me translate
his romantic words laced with profanities,
I can show you things no American can…
alternates sweet nothings with finger snaps to the staff.

He takes a restaurant postcard, rips it in half,
and writes a phone number on it in black marker
in case I have any trouble in the city I should call
collects his driver and heads off in his sleek black sedan,
ultimately alone, despite his best efforts
(but not likely to remain that way).

I still have the number,
I hold onto it like a talisman,
as if somehow by having it I can,
if the situation demands
summon
the General.

piroshki

if you don't know
(but you should, you must)
it's dough enclosing a filling
meat or vegetable or fungi
either baked or fried but as we know
fried is the pinnacle, fried is the guilty pleasure,
fried is what makes it heaven

you can get them everywhere in russia
street corners, little shops built off the sides
of buildings, train stations, cafes,
even higher-end restaurants where they try
to put a spin on what is an egalitarian dish
but no food designed to be held in one hand
and eaten with no utensils can be upper class

third place: omsk railway station, we had thirty
minutes before the train left, walked under seafoam walls,
found a café, ordered *piroshki* and took them onboard
warm dough and sautéed mushrooms, a hint of dill
when we finished, we watched scenery slide by,
chatted with a woman named lyutsia, short for *revolution*
on our way across the world, east to west

second place: srostki, the altai republic, speeding down
the chuyski trakt to mongolia, stopped at the huge roadside
market, where the *piroshki* look to be steroid-fed—
even split in half are too much for one person,
fried and stuffed with chopped hard-boiled egg and green onion,
we bought too many and tried too late to share them
while the vendors laughed and offered to sell us honey

first place: verhnaya beriozovka, outside ulan-ude,
we arrived in cool morning, toured the empty open-air
wooden architecture museum of historical log huts
she appeared as if summoned by mid-morning hunger
short buryat woman in a headscarf, bearing a white
enameled bucket covered by a clean blue cloth,
filled to the brim with hot, fresh, potato *piroshki*

for ten rubles, all of thirty-three cents, she sold
them all, still steaming, buttery enough
to satisfy julia child, she could have charged more
i bought the first and told my students
you must do this before i even took a bite
we were full and happy, she left with an empty
bucket but a filled purse, as if she'd satisfied all wishes

i believe in her, legendary baking-fairy of the steppe

The Galway Hobo

Ireland, 2009

He'd make a good Santa if his beard grew out. He always
returns to the spot on the stone pathway by the rushing Corrib,
just a little up from Jury's Inn, still within view of the bay
and the Burren mounding up to the south.

Only guessing he's a hobo, based on a track suit
that doesn't change, knitted cap, all-weather shoes, a
seeming lack of occupation besides staring at the water,
resting his arms on the black steel fence.

He spends most of his time looking at buildings, though
judging from the slow antics he performs, he got ahold
of a tai-chi instruction manual and checks his form
against the booklet open on the grass.

He's no drunk. At least, I've never seen him drinking,
he doesn't confront or engage, just ambles on his way,
but I warn my kids to keep their distance when they walk
to McIsaac's for milk or candy and cross his regular turf.

He never panhandles, like the Gypsy on Wolfe Tone bridge,
doesn't mutter like the wild-eyed dreadlocked man on Shop Street.
He's a fixture on the river, like grey herons or white swans,
the kayaking club surfing standing waves under O'Brien's bridge.

I build him a biography: he's royalty in disguise,
an unsung genius who haunts the downtown,
until one morning in December when the sunrise catches him
pissing against the wall.

The Gypsy Children in Orange

I have been warned. Guidebook
wisdom tells me how they wave dirty
scraps of unlined paper at me, words
I don't understand. This is France.
Why here, in the south, a minor station,
where few trains pass all day?
Perhaps they are stranded, left,
on their way to Paris to join
those at the gates of Versailles,
hoarse child-singers on the Metro,
mother crouched with grubby offspring
on the steps of Montmarte, as night
shadows fall on the Sacre-Coueur.
Dark men peddling golden chains,
six-foot long folding postcards.

The impudent one comes for me again.
I knock the paper away, it flutters down,
she curses at me in French. I respond
with nonsense syllables, she laughs.
No more trains through here tonight.
I stay across the street in a three-star
hotel I can't afford. Dinner? Only
deserted Sabbath streets. The proprietors
nod as the doors shut. There is nowhere
but their restaurant, a glass veranda
facing the stark railway station. I sit
under a Monet reproduction, away from
the glass so the children cannot see. I cut
the salty, white flesh with crossed silver
as they scream down the street to home.

On a Street in Dublin

He stepped into the Red Line *Luas* tram at Talbot Street,
thinking I was ahead of him as I bought tickets,
I came around the automat to a train gone, platform empty—
the incomprehensible tracked across my brain
I spun in place, denying eye's evidence
no eight-year old boy in a light blue raincoat
asked the old man in glasses and nicotine beard on the corner
but knowing his answer before he gave it.

Just off the fast ferry from Wales, out of Holyhead,
a weekend of castle-hunting, a trip for just the two of us,
I watched him sleep on the ferry over,
dash through shadowy Beaumaris passageways,
cool and deserted in the morning sun,
wave from the Conwy turrets and pose at Caernarvon,
tuck in to Welsh breakfasts (skipping the blood sausage),
catching train, bus, taxi, and steam rail in flawless autumn.

Because there is good in the world the female *Garda*
sits on her bicycle thirty yards away,
she'll pedal to Abbey Street to intercept the tram
and bring him back to me,
tears in his eyes, attack-hug to beat all hugs,
in ten minutes it will be over,
but while she streaks down the tracks
I run after her to the next stop, thinking too much.

Choking pain filling me that wasn't from
not enough air or the clenching of muscles
that if she is not there with him at the next stop,
if this doesn't come to an end he will use for his third
grade narrative project, then I want something else
I breathe, my shoes slipping between the cobblestones,
let me die now, let me die now, let me die now—
that will be better.

Night, Verbezhichi

2011

We are still on Moscow time,
but far from any city, as we
left Moscow with its fourteen million
to Lyudinovo with its forty thousand
to Verbezhichi with its uncounted,
but approximate, three hundred.

The roads are unpaved under eight inches
of fresh snow. It is January, and Russia
must live up to its stereotypes. The team bunks
with Praskovya Ivanovna, our host;
she shows us her funeral garments,
we play card games under the framed picture of her dead son.

The white-plastered sides of the massive brick stove
rise up to the left of my bed, head-high, pulsing
with heat after the morning stoking. Bits of ash fall down,
and I sweep them away before bedtime.
We made a snowman in the dark, right beside the gate,
to celebrate the New Year as the teapot whistled inside.

Andrei, Lena, Sergei, and Praskovya Ivanovna are sleeping,
in a few hours I will struggle up, victim of too many
glasses of tea, and stumble outside, past Vasya the pig,
the dogs and chickens, ducking under the net of clotheslines
(caught my head on one twice, but learned) to the outhouse,
flashlight in a freezing hand.

In that patch of courtyard the barn and house block the streetlight,
looking up I just see the stars, blazing cold, as my breath plumes.
You could stand there, waiting, listening, for a long time
without knowing it, like a pilot losing the horizon,
unaware until with a jerk you are back in the here and now.

Ten time zones away, barely dusk, my children sit down to dinner,
so that even if I called them we could not look up to the same sky,
could not share these winter stars, could not share this night.
I will drift back to sleep while someone smashes our snowman,
in the morning the Russians will tell me how I speak
English in my sleep, like a spy caught in the act.

the spark

i once toured the red october chocolate factory
in moscow on marsh island
before they turned it into high-end real estate,
artists studios, and late-night hangouts,
and on each production line everything whirred properly
whisked down through each step
clad in white smocks and caps they let us
reach into the clattering sequence
to sample sweets
until we were sick
but sometimes alongside each conveyor
product had left the line
flung itself outward onto the concrete
a wafer, uncovered in chocolate, not fully formed,
i used to think those rejects as the detritus
of industry, swept up and dumped in grey barrels
to be tossed as garbage,
though now i realize
they are poems
flung out of consciousness, the normal
pace of life as something attempting to be
wait—here comes another—
catch it before it is gone

About the Author

David Galloway turned to writing to fund his Russian dumpling habit, which takes him on sour cream-fueled binges to the motherland every year or so. Hanging with the babushkas, he assembles the impressions from his visits into a class, and a few people take it. Currently a professor of Russian at Hobart & William Smith Colleges, he grew up in suburban Maryland north of Baltimore. When he surfaces from fits of imagination, he usually finds himself in upstate New York, which is an excellent place to be.